The Story of
MOUNT RUSHMORE

By Marilyn Prolman

Illustrations by Phil Austin

CHILDRENS PRESS, CHICAGO

3 4 5 6 7 8 9 10 11 12 13 14 15 16 17 18 19 20 21 22 23 24 25 R 75

"That's a wonderful idea! I never would have thought of it," said Senator Peter Norbeck of South Dakota. Doane Robinson, the state historian, had just told him of his plan for a historical monument in the Black Hills. Mr. Robinson wanted an enormous figure carved on one of the large, granite peaks in the Black Hills area.

It was now the 1920's. Doane Robinson had thought about the monument for a long time. He loved the Black Hills region of the state. It was an area rich in history and legend. Many famous Indian warriors had lived and died in the shadow of its peaks. Calamity Jane and Wild Bill Hickok had lived there in frontier days. A memorial would make people familiar with this colorful history. It would also attract many visitors to South Dakota.

But carving a mountain was a large and expensive project. Robinson had come to ask Senator Norbeck for help. The Senator was well-liked by the people. He had worked very hard over the years to preserve the natural beauty of the Black Hills. He knew the area very well.

"I know just the place for the statue," said Norbeck excitedly. "The part of the mountains called 'The Needles.'" Robinson thought of these large granite shafts jutting into the air like cathedral spires. He agreed.

"Now we must present the idea to the people. Without their help this can't be done," said Robinson.

Soon stories appeared in the local newspapers throughout the state. "There is a definite plan to convert the Needles into massive and spectacular figures, symbolizing the history of the state," they reported.

Although some people liked the idea, many did not. They wrote letters to the newspapers protesting the carving. "Man makes statues, but God made the Needles. Let them alone," they said.

The people who lived in the Black Hills were especially unhappy. They did not like the idea of spoiling the natural beauty of the area. "The Needles should be left as Nature intended," they protested.

But criticism did not stop Doane Robinson. Instead, he became more determined to carry out his plan. He began to look for an artist who could perform such a large task. "The fellow who does it must be more than a stone carver," he said to Senator Norbeck.

The man he found was Gutzon Borglum. Borglum was impressed by the greatness of America. He wanted art in America to reflect that greatness. "We are living in an age of the colossal. Our age will some day be called the 'Colossal Age,'" he had once said.

When he heard what Robinson wanted him to do he was excited. He saw the possibility of making a

monument to all that America stood for. "I've always wanted to do something big," he said, "remodel a state or make over a mountain range, something like that. This is my chance."

Borglum had just left a big project in Atlanta, Georgia. He had been carving an enormous memorial to Robert E. Lee into the side of Stone Mountain. Unfortunately, Borglum had a bad temper. After getting into an argument with the people who had hired him, he had smashed the models for his mountain sculpture and fled the state. When Robinson wrote him, he was actually a fugitive from Georgia justice.

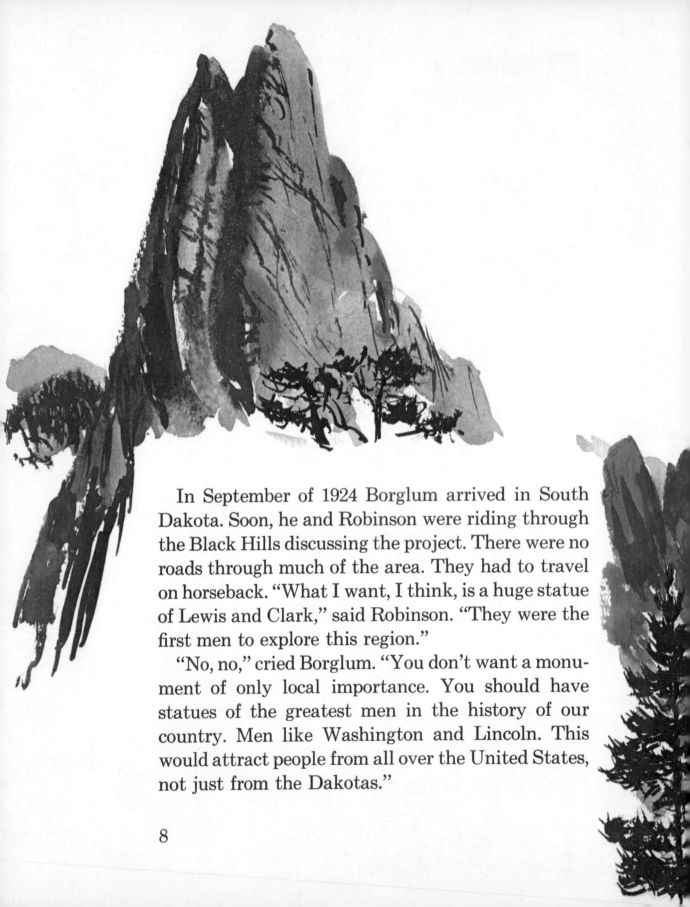

In September of 1924 Borglum arrived in South Dakota. Soon, he and Robinson were riding through the Black Hills discussing the project. There were no roads through much of the area. They had to travel on horseback. "What I want, I think, is a huge statue of Lewis and Clark," said Robinson. "They were the first men to explore this region."

"No, no," cried Borglum. "You don't want a monument of only local importance. You should have statues of the greatest men in the history of our country. Men like Washington and Lincoln. This would attract people from all over the United States, not just from the Dakotas."

8

Robinson thought for a minute. "Yes, you're probably right," he admitted.

"Probably!" thundered Borglum. "Of course I'm right!"

They rode through the area of the Needles, the place that Senator Norbeck had suggested for the carving.

"Stop!" ordered Borglum.

He dismounted and began to climb to a higher point of ground. Robinson followed. Finally Borglum reached a place from which he could get a good view of the granite spires. "Yes!" he exclaimed. "I see Washington carved into one spire and Lincoln carved into another."

They returned to their horses and rode on. Soon they were in a region of great granite mountains. Borglum looked around him.

"I've changed my mind," he said to Robinson. "I would like to see the whole side of a mountain carved with figures larger than any others yet carved in this country. I want to find a higher place where the work will be safe now and for millions of years to come."

Robinson was stunned. He had not thought of anything so big or so expensive. But, he was still enthusiastic. He knew it would be one of the finest monuments in the world when it was finished.

Borglum generated excitement wherever he went. People began to change their minds about the monument. "It may not be such a crazy scheme after all," they said. Borglum talked to those who still thought the Needles were going to be carved. He assured them that they wouldn't be touched. "I have no intention of making totem poles out of these wonderful spires."

Robinson and Norbeck went on planning. The Black Hills were located on government land. Permission to do the carving had to be granted by Congress. But most important, money had to be collected. Senator Norbeck went to Washington and presented the plan to the men in the Senate. They agreed to the carving. They also promised that if the citizens of South Dakota would give money for the memorial, the government would give money too.

Meanwhile, Borglum made another trip through the Black Hills. He camped out and explored the area. He climbed over the cliffs, carefully examining the rock. "I must find exactly the right place for the sculpture," he thought.

One day Borglum saw just the spot he had been looking for. It was a giant granite cliff towering well above the peaks around it. It faced southeast. The sun would shine on it most of the day. And the rock was solid. The name of the peak was Mount Rushmore. "This is the playground of the gods," he said to the men who were with him.

Borglum climbed to the top. There he lay on his back and looked up at the blue sky. "We will put history on this mountain," he said.

Borglum was anxious to get to work. He began hiring people and getting the mountainside ready for the carving. A small road was cleared through the trees at the base of the mountain. Trucks thundered down the road, delivering special equipment.

Borglum arranged a spectacular dedication ceremony at Mount Rushmore to mark the beginning of the carving. He placed ads in all the local newspapers saying, "Those who stay at home will miss the opportunity to participate in one of the greatest events in the history of the state." Few people could resist an invitation like that. On August 10, 1927, thousands turned out for the dedication.

The main speaker of the day was President Calvin Coolidge. He wore cowboy boots and a ten-gallon hat for the occasion. "We have come here to dedicate a cornerstone that was laid by the hand of the Almighty," he began the ceremony.

There were no cannon available. Instead, they blasted twenty-one tree stumps off the mountain for a presidential salute. Then, flag after flag was raised to symbolize each nation that had claimed ownership of the area since colonial times. Each flag represented a different country. A Sioux Indian in full dress and townspeople wearing French, Spanish, and colonial costumes took part.

At the conclusion of the ceremony, President Coolidge handed Borglum four drills. Solemnly Borglum climbed to the top of Mount Rushmore. The crowd watched in amazement as Borglum was lowered over the side of the mountain to do the first drilling. When he returned to the platform, he handed one drill to the President, one to Doane Robinson, and one to Senator Norbeck. He kept the fourth drill for himself.

The dedication was a great success. People from all over the state sent money to support the memorial. Work began soon after that. Daily reports were circulated with the slogan "RUSH MORE."

First a long, winding, wooden stairway was built to the top of the mountain. Later it was replaced by a cable car. At the top a workshop, a dynamite storeroom, and a lunchroom were built. At the base of the mountain, workers built a studio, a blacksmith's shop, a bunkhouse, a restaurant, and a custodian's house.

Meanwhile, Borglum continued to work on the models for the figures. By this time the plan called for the heads of George Washington, Thomas Jefferson, Abraham Lincoln, and Theodore Roosevelt. Each of these men had dramatically contributed to the destiny of the United States.

Borglum first shaped the figures in clay. Then he made larger models from a mixture of plaster of Paris and wood shavings. These were five feet high. The finished sculpture would be twelve times that, as high as a five-story building.

To get himself and his men over the side of the mountain, Borglum invented "swing seats." These were leather-covered steel seats attached to harnesses. Steel cables from the top of the mountain were connected to the harnesses. The men were able to move their arms freely. They could also use their feet to push off from the rock and swing themselves from one place to another.

The carving was divided into a series of steps. The first step was called "pointing." Each of the heads was drawn on special paper marked off in one-inch squares. At every point the workmen could be shown the exact location for putting in the drills and the exact depth to which the drills were to go.

These charts had to be very precise because the sculpture was so large. From a swing seat on the mountain it was impossible for a man to see anything but the one area he was working on. If a man worked on the left eye, he could not see the work on the right eye, the hairline, or the lower lip. But with each man following the directions on the pointing chart, the sculpture began to take shape. Because of the enormous size of the faces, most of the carving was done by blasting away large sections of rock with dynamite.

"Mistakes cannot be corrected!" Borglum warned the men. "There must be no mistakes." Carefully they drilled holes to exactly the depth indicated

16

on the charts. Then they filled the holes with exactly the right amount of dynamite.

Twice a day at noon and at 4:00 P.M., the men stopped work and returned to their camp at the base of the mountain. When everyone was safely off the mountain, the dynamite charges were set off. By the time the memorial was finished, 450,000 tons of broken granite lay at the base of the mountain.

In 1930 the first face was finished. For months everyone had been waiting to see what would finally appear on the mountain. Another colorful ceremony was planned.

On July 4, a large crowd gathered at the base of Mount Rushmore. A 72-foot flag covered the sculpture. The crowd waited impatiently for the flag to be removed.

Speeches were made, planes flew overhead, and a message from President Herbert Hoover was read.

Finally the time came. Riflemen fired. The flag was taken away. There, on the mountain, was the 60-foot face of George Washington.

At first the crowd was silent. Then everyone burst into applause. Cheers were heard from all sides. "Amazing! I can't believe it!" they cried.

The monument was a great success. Newspapers all over the country printed stories about it. Visitors started coming regularly to Mount Rushmore.

More money was needed to continue the carving. Again Senator Norbeck went to Washington to ask Congress for help. At first they refused. "The money should be raised in South Dakota," they said. "This is a state project."

"No," Norbeck answered. "This is a monument not just to four men but to the ideals of the whole

nation. It has already attracted thousands of visitors from all over the country, and it is not even half finished." Congress granted more money.

Borglum began carving the head of Thomas Jefferson. It was placed to the left of Washington. One day, a workman came to Borglum and said, "There are too many cracks in the stone. We will have to blast this face away and start somewhere else."

Jefferson was moved to the right of Washington, but again there were flaws in the granite. Everywhere Borglum wanted to place the nose, a crack

appeared. He was very angry. "Every time I find a large crack, I must make a new model of the face," he said.

Flaws in the rock had to be avoided at all costs. Even a small crack would widen year after year. Water that collected in the crack during the fall would freeze in winter and expand. Sections of rock would fall off. After hundreds of years the nose could split wide open. "I have no intention of leaving a head on that mountain that in the course of 500 or 5,000 years will be without a nose," Borglum said.

Finally Borglum solved the problem. He changed the position of the Jefferson head one last time. The crack that appeared was not as deep as the others. He was able to fill it with a mixture of white lead and granite dust.

At last the face of Jefferson was ready to be unveiled. Borglum heard that President Franklin Delano Roosevelt would be in the area. He invited the President to come to Mount Rushmore.

"The President will come to see your memorial," his secretary said, "but he will not have time to speak."

Plans were quickly made for another dedication. Borglum greeted President Roosevelt at the base of the mountain. Then, at Borglum's signal, there was a blast of dynamite. The 72-foot flag was removed from Jefferson's face. Borglum asked the President to dedicate the monument as a shrine of democracy.

The president's secretary jumped between the two men. He said angrily, "I told you before, the President will not speak."

But Roosevelt said, "I've changed my mind. I believe I must say something after all. I had no idea of the beauty and importance of this memorial until ten minutes ago." Then President Roosevelt turned to the crowd. He told them that the monument was an inspiration to continue the democratic form of government, not only in the United States, but also throughout the world.

The audience cheered. Borglum, Robinson, and Senator Norbeck were very proud. They had impressed the President of the United States. Their monument was a success.

Time and time again those who had been against the project changed their minds when they saw it. In 1934 more than 150,000 people saw the partly finished work. When more money was needed for the carving, one member of the House of Representatives told his fellow congressmen, "Every doubt and question will melt into nothingness if you will visit Mount Rushmore and see the memorial itself."

Money continued to be a problem. Again and again Borglum and Robinson had to ask for more. "This will be enough to finish the memorial," Borglum would say. But then he would add things to the plan. More money was always necessary.

Borglum's first plan for the memorial included only three figures—Washington, Jefferson, and Lincoln. Then Theodore Roosevelt was added. Borglum also wanted to carve an inscription into the mountain beside the four faces. This was to be a 600-word history of the United States. President Coolidge had written it, but it was never used.

Borglum's next idea was to build a Hall of Records. He wanted to carve an enormous room into the granite of the mountain. Its entrance would be 140 feet high. It would have a glass door 12 feet wide and 20 feet high. The room would hold all the historical records of the United States. All these plans had to wait, while the work on Lincoln's face went on.

In September of 1937, the time came to unveil the

head of Lincoln. The event was broadcast all over the country on the radio.

The Lincoln face was as spectacular as the others. The sparkle in Lincoln's eye was reflected from a sculptured granite block 30 inches long. Lincoln's lower lip was 18 feet wide. The mole on his cheek was 16 inches long.

The most memorable comment of the day was given by a little-known radio announcer.

"Next to Jefferson," he said, "is a space which, in a few years, will reveal the face of our President, Franklin Delano Roosevelt."

The crowd gasped. Shouts of "Theodore Roosevelt!" "Teddy!" came from the crowd. By this time everyone knew that Theodore Roosevelt was to be the fourth man on the mountain.

The face of Theodore Roosevelt was the last to be carved on Mount Rushmore. Some people objected to adding him to the memorial. They did not think he was as important as the other three men. But despite these protests, Borglum went ahead with the carving. When the Roosevelt head was unveiled in 1939, more than 12,000 people came to the ceremony.

Now the job seemed to be almost done. Everyone thought that the four faces were a splendid achievement. Very few people were interested in building the Hall of Records. The memorial had already cost twice as much as had been planned. Almost a million dollars had been spent. Most of the money had come from the federal government, but the people had also contributed.

It had taken fourteen years to carve the mountain. Borglum had said it would only take five. But every time the money ran out or the temperature fell below zero, the work had to stop.

Borglum had not been an easy man to work for. He fired his secretary many times; but she always came back the next day as if nothing had happened. One workman boasted, "I was fired and rehired by Borglum eight times in fourteen years."

Although the work had been very dangerous, not a single life had been lost. Only two accidents occurred. Once lightning struck an electric power

line that led to the mountain. Two men received shocks, and one man had his shoes blown off. Another time, a cable car went out of control. Fortunately, the men inside the car were able to slow it down. Only the man who jumped out was hurt. He recovered and went back to work on the mountain.

When the work was in its final stages, the state of South Dakota built a special road leading to the memorial. This made it easier for visitors to come to the mountain. Senator Norbeck planned the road so that people could approach Mount Rushmore from its best side. He had walked over the area twenty times to work out this route.

The road circles around Iron Mountain, several miles away from the memorial. In some places the road goes through tunnels cut into the mountain. Each tunnel entrance faces Mount Rushmore. Through these natural picture frames visitors can see spectacular views of the four faces.

The Mount Rushmore National Memorial stands in the Black Hills for all to see. It is not a monument to four men. It is the symbol of a nation. It will last for some five million years.

George Washington represents the founding of the country. He guided the writing of the Constitution. Washington stands for the spirit of independence that caused the United States to break away from Great Britain.

Thomas Jefferson represents America's faith in the common man. It is the common man who has made this country great. Jefferson wrote the Declaration of Independence, based upon the idea that all men are created equal.

Abraham Lincoln stands for the fight against slavery and the preservation of the Union. He, above all, was responsible for keeping the nation together.

Theodore Roosevelt is the fourth figure. His personality was most like the soul of America. He was full of restless energy and the progressive spirit. The dream of joining East and West began with Columbus. It became a reality when Roosevelt built the Panama Canal.

Together these four men form a memorial to the history and greatness of the United States.

About the Author: Marilyn Prolman was born in Boston, Massachusetts. She attended the University of Wisconsin where she majored in English. She is a free-lance writer and has worked for several publishers and public relations firms in Chicago. A mid-westerner by choice, she has lived in Chicago since her graduation.

About the Artist: Phil Austin has devoted his life to art. He studied at the University of Michigan and at the Academy of Art in Chicago. He chose watercolor as his favorite medium because of its sparkle and speed of execution, making it possible to capture the momentary happenings and passing moods in nature. His paintings have been exhibited at a number of galleries throughout the country and Vincent Price has purchased a number of his works for the Sears Collection. He is the father of five children and lives in Waukegan, Illinois.